SWEETLIGHT

Canyon de Chelly
The Timeless Fold

by

Conger Beasley, Jr.
Photography by Mary S. Watkins

SWEETLIGHT BOOKS
Arcata, California

Canyon de Chelly
The Timeless Fold

Published by: SWEETLIGHT BOOKS
P.O. Box 307
Arcata, CA 95521

Datura photo courtesy of National Park Service. Typeset in Baskerville by Pioneer Graphics of Eureka, California.

Library of Congress Catalog Card Number: 88-60604
ISBN: 0-9604462-4-9

Manufactured in the USA.
First Printing 1988.

"What's the use of writing at all unless imaginatively? Unless one's vision can lend something to a thing, there's small reason in proceeding to proclaim one has seen it. Mere looking *everyone can do for himself."*

– Henry James

"Touch is relative but sight is oblong."

– Guillaume Apollinaire

for Jim Murfin
1929–1987

Contents

"*I'm sitting under a cottonwood tree...*"

I'm sitting under a cottonwood tree across from White House Ruin. It's the last day of September... a warm day, the sun shining brightly, filling the narrow canyon with light. The wall above the ruin rises in a convex arc hundreds of feet to the rim. From this point—at the bottom of the canyon—the rim looks jagged and distant. Composed of Shinarump Conglomerate, a thin sedimentary layer deposited some 170 million years ago, the rim, much of which has eroded away, sits on top of a thick deposit of de Chelly (pronounced *du SHAY*) sandstone. Formed around 230 million years ago, the sandstone descends in sheer walls to the canyon floor. Pink in

1

color, roseate in places, darkening in late afternoon, the walls on warm evenings glow with a deep umber refulgence. At all times, even on moonless nights, the walls reflect some kind of color, stored energy from the sun.

The walls seem to swell and pulse with radiance, expanding to accommodate light during the day, giving off a residual glow at night...sentient rock with a lifebeat of its own. When I press my cheek against the smooth, rippleless surface I feel a pleasant warmth. The wall is a vast, soaring palette against which the chemical interaction of water dripping over the surface leaves tailing streaks hundreds of feet long...dark, inky draperies that form no discernible pattern, but that impinge upon the consciousness in mystifying ways.

Cottonwood tree and canyon wall

"*It feels like summer down here. . .*"

It feels like summer down here. The intense heat of August is gone, though outside the shade, in the sunlight, it is hot. I have ventured down here for several reasons, one of which is to say goodbye to the sun. Tomorrow is the first of October. We have already passed the equinox, and the sun is fading. A week ago (speaking in Ptolemaic configurations), it drifted over the equator toward the Tropic of Capricorn.

The ultimate fear among primitive peoples was total darkness. The sun was the source of light and growth; any diminution of it aroused terrible anxieties. In the fall, when the light began to wane, there was great concern that it would not return. Elaborate devices were constructed (Stonehenge-type measuring tools) to chart the sun's descent to the southern horizon. After the solstice, how anxious people must have been to discover proof that the sun was actually on its way back. By inventing measuring devices to track its return, early man was able to visualize the cosmos as a geometric form which helped give coherence to a life he secretly feared was chaotic and meaningless.

To ensure the sun's return, the Aztecs ripped the hearts from the chests of thousands of victims, held those hearts up, gushing blood, to the sun. The difference between now and then is antipodal. Today, the sun functions as an adjunct to our pleasures—something to ''purchase'' for a few hours or days to increase our attractiveness, augment our self-esteem. The sun has become a commodity, held in reserve for special occasions, which we take down at will, twist open, and splash on our cheeks.

And so goodbye. It will be months before I feel its warmth again. The prospect depresses me. Goodbye goodbye goodbye. I have said goodbye to the sun many times before, always with regret, always with a twinge of sadness. What can I do during the dark months ahead to ensure its return? What prayers can I offer, what talismans of hope? Come December, at the time of the solstice, I will journey to a secluded spot, face south, and make supplicatory gestures to induce it to return. As the light grows (hopefully) brighter, I will trace its path back to this hemisphere along subtle whorls grooved out of fields of stone.

White House Ruin

How old is White House Ruin? Nobody really knows. An educated guess is that it was built sometime during the 12th century. Back then it stood taller, two, three, even four pueblo stories, towering up to the level of the dark niche in the canyon wall that opens above it like a cave. The dwellings inside probably went all the way up to the slanted ceiling. In times of danger the people in the pueblos below could climb up into the niche, pull their ladders behind them, and defend themselves from there.

Several walls were built of white masonry, an architectural style thought to have originated in Chaco Canyon, 100 miles away in New Mexico. (A much larger community lived there, leaving several aggregations of spectacular ruins, the most extensive anywhere north of Mexico.) Sunlight beaming over the south rim of Canyon de Chelly pierced a small aperture in the pueblo wall and illuminated the room. The white walls refracted the light and diffused it. A ray of sunlight, poking into the murky interior, magically dispelled the gloom.

Anasazi ("someone's ancestors")—afflicted with rickets, cataracts, rheumatism—felt the healing power of the sun in their bones like a medieval alchemist the touch of liquid gold against his fingers. It was their elixir, generator of corn and squash and beans in the modest plots along the river below their pueblo houses. Sunlight winging through a narrow opening worked upon their consciousness in amazing ways. The effect was to lift them out of their square rooms, the canyon's narrow width, like a wave of warm air rising off the bottom. It made them airborne, not in the manner of wheeling ravens, but mentally buoyant. Down in the depths the light became their horizon, a vista that kept at a tolerable distance the claustrophobic thickness of the walls.

White House Ruin

"*The sound of sheep baaing...*"

The sound of sheep baaing from somewhere downstream blats against my ears. Sound travels laterally along these sheer walls, around bends, despite the presence of numerous trees, with astounding clarity and ease. The sound follows the track of the canyon wall, and no matter which way the wall twists, the sound glides smoothly along it like an invisible snake.

"What does this country mean to me..."

What does this country mean to me or any *belagana*? Kit Carson on the subject was never very eloquent. The esthetics of landscape hardly interested him. He reported what he saw in a terse, perfunctory tone. In the winter of 1863-64 he came out to Canyon de Chelly with a small army to compel the Navajos to leave. Under orders from General Carleton—a pious, fanatical Indian-hater—Carson burned peach orchards and hogans, slaughtered sheep and cattle, trampled corn and squash patches. At the base of Fortress Rock, deep inside the canyon, he waited patiently until the defenders, limp with hunger, came down and surrendered. He killed every Navajo warrior he found. His orders were to corral the entire nation and march it east to New Mexico. The question remains: What does this country mean to a white person? We come into it, sit awhile, look around, snap a few pictures, and leave.

It takes a long time for country to soak in. We live mostly as strangers to the turf we occupy. Farmers who till the soil we deem closest to Nature, but even their vision is limited by the vagaries of weather and crop yield. What of those who seek to disappear into a landscape? Who long to orient their instincts to the features of a particular topography? Where do they belong? What do they have to say?

Geology

Approaching by car from the west, you see the
formation, a rounded hump like a turtle shell, rising
up off the plain. The Defiance Uplift, 30 to 40 miles
wide, stretches 100 miles in a north-south direction
along the Arizona-New Mexico border. Fifty million
years ago, at the close of the Cretaceous Period, the
land rose slowly. Streams flooding west out of the
Chuska Mountains cut down through the rising
crust, much like knives held level against the surface
of an expanding cake. The streams maintained their
courses, and over the millenia sliced deep ravines out
of the terrain. Tight frost cracked the rocks, tree
roots gouged the cracks, raindrops smoothed the

edges, chunks of land broke off and tumbled down to lower ground. Weathered by wind and water, these pieces fractured into smaller segments, which in turn were washed toward the sea.

First There Was
the Dream

The first time I came here a strange thing occurred. Cooper and I had driven up from Flagstaff, a leisurely route that took us first to Grand Canyon then to the Four Corners and then down to Canyon de Chelly. It was early April; the nights were chilly, the sun warm—with a newly minted brightness—at midday. Late one afternoon we drove through the town of Chinle and chugged up the west slope of the uplift. At Spider Rock Overlook we parked the car and walked to the rim. The sun was low, the canyon floor engulfed in shadows, but a few burning rays still illuminated the upper portion of Spider Rock monolith. We found a place close to the rim, under a

Spider Rock

rocky outcropping, where we could sit and watch the interplay of light and shadow. Behind us a wind stirred the stunted piñons. We sat awhile, talking. We were the only ones there. A few patches of snow lingered in the shadows under the rocks. Winter still hung over the canyon, but lightly, like a cloud on the verge of dissolving; the air was cold but not uncomfortable. Cooper was telling me about something he had done when a violet-green swallow buzzed between us, so close it stirred the air, its narrow wings making a distinct rasping sound. The hair prickled on the back of my neck. I had heard the sound of those wingbeats recently in a dream. The exact same sound.

The dream had been vivid. A three-story house, built out of limerock slabs and shrouded with dense ivy, stood before me. It was night, a wet night; in fact, it had just ceased raining. The front lawn was damp and soggy. A few drops plinked audibly against the ivy. I looked up at a dormer window projecting from the sloping roof. With rapid arm beats I rose up past the front door and second-story windows to the dormer. I nudged my face against the shutters and felt them melt inward to a kind of gritty darkness. An ominous humming greeted my ears. Inside the attic I could discern the dim outline of figures that glowed in the dark as if dusted with metallic pollen.

Even though I couldn't recognize the faces, I knew who they were: My mother and grandmother, dead these many years, yet somehow attentive to my presence, waiting.

An alarm sounded in my head. You don't want to be here now, a voice declared. Hastily I pulled back, banging my head against the window. I popped free, and flapping my arms excitedly, soared up over the roof to the other side of the house. How dreams can alter in composition in the space of an instant! A city congealed into view, like a spill of tar-colored gruel sparked with aluminum flecks. The backyard sloped to the edge of the cliff. The yard was cross-hatched with sidewalks leading to classrooms. The backyard expanded in size to become the campus of an urban university that at this strange hour was dimly lit with warm blue lights. Along one of these walks marched a tall, attractive woman, cradling books against her chest. Now for some fun, I thought, and started down on a low, hurtling slant like a fighter on a strafing run. The wind brisked my cheeks; my arm/wings made a distinct *fooming* sound.

The woman looked up, her face contorting in terror, and uttered a piercing scream. Her books tumbled to the ground. A pang of remorse shuddered through me. I hadn't meant to come on so strong.

The night was weird, and I was in a playful mood. With a chortle I shot up over the trees at the edge of the cliff, my arm/wings still *foom*ing, then out over the city.

The dream appeared one night in Florida as I slept high up in a tall condominium within earshot of the grumbling Atlantic. A month later, sitting on the rim of Canyon de Chelly, watching the last orange rays of the fading sun flee up the walls out of reach of a mass of solid shadow, a violet-green swallow (*Tachycineta thalassina*) buzzed past my ear, *foom*ing unmistakably, its white belly flashing, before plunging out of sight. The energy of all the natural forces in the world seemed to pause for one rarefied second. The sound was unmistakable, the same as in the dream, a diving sound, quick and cutting; I felt myself being pulled away from my safe perch out into the abyss that opened at my feet.

In the car on the way back to Chinle I tried to reproduce with my voice the sound that the bird had made. Cooper looked at me curiously. "It's hard to explain," I said, "but I'll try."

I told him the story. He stroked his well-trimmed beard. "Interesting," he agreed. "The archetypal women in your life, waiting patiently, even though you're not ready to join them. It's good to know. A glimpse, maybe, of a world beyond this world."

19

He paused and drummed his fingers against the steering wheel. "Or a world that runs alongside this one in secret."

The darkness seemed to rise off the uplift like a coroner's shroud. A faint orange smear colored the western horizon. First there was the dream, I thought. And now this. The actual sound. This version of it as experienced by my physical senses. Images like waves lapping ceaselessly against my consciousness. Where do they come from? Where do they finally roll to?

"That bird is what I am," I declared. "It is what I was. It is what I will become again."

Cooper grinned and doubled up his fist and pumped it once. The car glided on down the slope.

Trees

Cottonwood, tamarisk, Russian olive. The last two, introduced in the late 1800s, have taken firm hold on the canyon floor. White House Trail down from the rim passes under a canopy of olive trees. The branches form a bower, a shaded region of drowsy repose. It might be fun to sleep there some night. Like a rabbit, under a leafy, protective dome.

"*The sound of sheep grows louder...*"

The sound of sheep grows louder. They must be coming up the canyon, maybe to graze in the meadow behind where I sit, a narrow field between the trees and canyon wall. They make a powerful racket, bawling and crying and nagging. The sound slides along the walls, filling my ears, enveloping me in an invisible nimbus. I imagine them bunched together in a tight mass, woolly bodies bobbing up and down, chaperoned by a lone Navajo and a dog.

Navajo woman

The Moon Lily

Yesterday, near Junction Rock, I saw two datura plants, their soft white petals open to the sun despite the lateness of the hour. Datura are wary of daylight, and usually fold their blossoms by mid-morning. They prefer moonlight, the glow that sun-drenched rocks give off after dark.

Desert Indians ingest portions of the plant for ceremonial purposes. Every part of the plant, including the root, contains alkaloids, notably atropine. Every part of the plant, whether taken in large quantities or small, can induce hallucinations.

Datura flourishes in sandy or gravelly terrain below 4,000 feet. It is common in sagebrush scrub,

Datura

desert and foothills and canyons, from California to Texas, and down into South America. One Indian name, *tolquacha*, is from the Aztec word *toloatzin*: "to bow the head in respect."

Hopi use datura to cure a person of "meanness." When consumed in a fire and the fumes inhaled, it can aid respiration. Used as a poultice, the plant salves burns and sores. Merely rubbing the eyes after pulling the leaves off the stem can cause the pupils to dilate. When eaten in quantity, visual distortion can result, flushed skin, rapid heartbeat, physical convulsions, and death.

Browsing animals, repelled by the taste and odor, refuse to eat it. The large, bell-shaped flowers grow singly on long stems, and are pollinated by sphinx moths that come at night to sip the nectar. The petals exude a fragrant scent; when the leaves are bruised they give off a fetid odor.

The plant is thought to act more forcefully upon the brain than belladonna or henbane. In India, assassins used it to dispatch their victims. The priests of Apollo at Delphi ate datura to assist them in making prophecies.

Other names: Thornapple, Devil's Apple, Jimson Weed, Stinkweed, Devil's Trumpet, Apple of Peru, Dream Weed, the Moon Lily.

A member of the potato family.

The Anglo from Albuquerque

An Anglo from Albuquerque came out to Canyon de Chelly with the express purpose of committing suicide. Unfortunately, he couldn't bring himself to jump off the rim at any of the overlooks. He thought about drowning, but the time was early August and there was barely enough water in the Rio de Chelly to wet his lips. However, he was a determined man. His life was a mess, he was beset by a nagging anxiety that gnawed at his bowels like a rat. Upon leaving the canyon, he stomped the accelerator of his car and rammed head-on into an oil truck on the highway outside Chinle. On the rim, with the scent of piñon pine in his nostrils, gazing down upon the

Canyon de Chelly

bucolic scene, he couldn't muster the nerve to step off. The other way—enveloped in a familiar metal cocoon—he felt more confident; *he knew what to do*.

"Chiching"

As products of American civilization we bring to
                  places like this
lots of mental garbage
    Junk   Dross   Sludge   Babblegook
bits of refuse   registered by adhesive minds,
    chaff of excessive information glut
dataspew manufactured by quantification junkies
that buzzes mercilessly inside our brains
forming an obstruction between ourselves
& the objects we regard ,   muddling our response
garbling the transfer of energy & light.
"Chiching" a philosopher once called it,
nervy kinetic *surface* hum

we acquire from being daily bombarded
by electronic crackles   ,   the "bim-bim"
                    Steppenwolf lamented
    & work'd diligently to exorcise
like a Puritan magistrate
the subtle, corrosive presence of Satan
in every tree   in every leaf

                    •

The same industrial genius that produced tanks &
                            Liberty ships
in WW2
refrigerators & chrome-slab'd cars in the 1950s
today cranks out meaningless "newsworthy" units
                            that dissolve
upon the tongue like cotton candy
leaving a sweet cloying taste that contributes
to the build-up of fatty deposits
in the arteries of our dutiful, hard-working hearts.

Sibelius in Hopiland

One time, driving northeast through Hopiland toward Canyon de Chelly, we picked up a classical station from Flagstaff and listened to the sonorous final movement of Sibelius's Second Symphony transmitted along a crackling wave length with the sun low behind us casting gaunt, elongated shadows out of every gully and draw, and Black Mesa looming to our left, its pine-clad slopes already shrouded in murky darkness. Across a million miles of space and time came these measured cadences, solid blocks of sound carefully smoothed and rounded and thoughtfully stacked on top of one another, peaking finally in a stately crescendo that raised the hackles on our arms and brought a whoop of delight to our lips. Images of dark forests, pitch-scented and stirred by sharp Arctic winds, clouded our minds, while simultaneously, gazing out the window, we viewed a vastly different terrain, blotched and peeled as a buzzard's neck, with a horizon that ached for definition. The music recalled the fact that this land had once been deeply forested with lush ferns and broad-leafed plants. . . a dark, humid terrain located much closer to the equator. What we were viewing now, eons later, were the bleached bones, the fossilized embers, of a once flourishing tropical life; turned inside out, as it were, by the passage of time. . . yin transformed into yang, fire into ice, liquid into stubble by the rumble of plate tectonics, the grind of continental drift. And binding it all together (spanning the eons!) was this sturdy musical utterance, these steely, arching, *architectural* cadences coming to us over a sputtery radio wave on the edge of Hopiland, with the Defiance Uplift clearly visible to the east, Black Mesa to the north. Sibelius, boon composer, engendering image upon image, a mix of imaginative pictures, collectively retained in our consciousness, like miniature, overlapping continents. . . Pangaea to all our hopes and sorrows.

Canyon del Muerto

Lieutenant Narbona was pissed. All day his troops had tried to dislodge a group of Navajos holed up in a cave high up on the canyon wall. Supported by sharpshooters down below, the soldiers had struggled up a steep talus slope to within 200 feet of the cave rim. Only a few junipers offered them protection from a blizzard of Navajo rocks and arrows. The sharpshooters directed a heavy stream of fire at the roof of the cave, trying to deflect the bullets and cause havoc among the defenders. The Spaniards didn't know how many people were up there, whether they were warriors or women and children; they only knew that Lieutenant Narbona wanted them out of the way.

Pictograph of Narbona expedition

It was a long day. The weather was cold. Winter in Canyon de Chelly can be bitter, and this day in January 1805 was no exception. For weeks Narbona and 300 Spanish soldiers had been looking for Navajos to kill. Early in January they entered the canyon down a narrow defile at the head of its northeast arm. The Indians were elusive, the terrain well-suited to ambush and defense.

The cave was actually a lookout used to detect the presence of Ute raiders. The Spaniards would have missed it had not 1) an old woman jeered at them as they passed along the canyon floor; or 2) a disgruntled lover, spurned by a chieftain while seeking the hand of a woman in the chieftain's clan, tipped them off as to the cave's whereabouts. Nearly a hundred people, mainly women, children, and old folks, were packed inside. The main force of Navajo warriors was positioned on top of the opposite rim. During the day they filtered down into the canyon and harassed the Spanish flanks but were unable to distract them. Lieutenant Narbona was convinced that the main body of Navajo warriors was holed up in the cave some 600 feet above the canyon floor.

From the top of the talus slope the wall rose 200 feet to the cave in a sheer climb. Night fell early; suffering miserably from the cold, Narbona's men bedded down as best they could between the rocks and junipers. Next morning, as sharpshooters sent up a deadly fire (Narbona later reported that his men had expended more than 10,000 rounds of ammunition; this, in the days of muzzle-loading rifles.), the Spaniards single file climbed up the ancient footholds notched out of sandstone by the Anasazi. The first soldier over the rock parapet was greeted by a woman who thrust a stone knife into his guts. The soldier grabbed her by the neck; clawing wildly, shrieking with rage and pain, they reeled off the rim and tumbled to their deaths.

The few rocks and knives and arrows the defenders had left simply weren't enough to stave off the Spanish rush. Ricocheting musket balls had devastated their numbers; with clubs, swords, and buckshot—in an orgy of slaughter—the soldiers dispatched the rest. The only survivor, an old man, escaped detection by hiding under a stack of corpses. The dead were left to rot; their bones still molder in the cave. Lieutenant Narbona was pleased; he felt he had won a significant victory. In order to achieve some kind of tally, he ordered his men to cut off the ears of the dead. To his superior down in Sonora he wrote, ''The Corporal Baltasar is bringing eighty-four pairs of ears and the six that are lacking to complete the ninety.''

"*The sheep draw near...*"

The sheep draw near. Their bawling fills the air. The sound bounces off the smooth canyon walls.

I put down my notebook, stand up, cross the sand, wade into the river. Another sound, arching over the sheep, catches my ear. Human voices imitating the agitated sheep. Mocking their plaintive cries—nagging, whining, bleating. The sun, close to the rim now, shines directly in my eyes, spangling the brown current.

The sheep cross downstream, accompanied by a man on horseback wearing a dark shirt. Another man, on foot, carrying a long switch, follows the herd, flicking the tip at strays.

The sheep cross the river to the pasture behind the cottonwood trees. Dust motes, insects, birds whirl through the brilliant sliver of light that flangs off the water. The sun, poised above the rim, dazzles my eyes. A murky current slops my ankles. I lean back against the heated sandstone cliff, turn my face downstream toward the noisy sheep, feel the sun congeal across my flesh like a balming oil.

A dragonfly skims my forehead with its papery wings.

Little Anasazi

Tiny incandescent particles flutter thru the air
—little Anasazi ,   clad in loincloths
dangling from parachutes

descend slowly to earth

"Cottonwood leaves..."

Cottonwood leaves chidder over my head. Quintessential western tree, it flourishes along watercourses. A greedy organism, its roots push deep to tap the water table. Despite its thirst, the Fremont cottonwood never grows very tall—certainly not as tall as a sycamore; however, it grows quickly and plentifully.

Heart-shaped leaves, smooth and shiny green. A flat stem enables the leaf to twist 180 degrees in a slight breeze. In summer the leaves make a soft, lathery sound. This afternoon the sound is sharp and crisp. The bands of heat that in summer layer the canyon floor have disappeared. The air is dry, almost brittle. It coats my skin like cellophane. The sun, slipping toward the south, draws the warmth and moisture with it. Soon the canyon will be bare and lifeless, the trees stripped of leaves. The walls will constrict and fold in upon themselves like the paws of a hibernating animal.

Cottonwood leaves

Navajo Mother

She was walking along the highway, 20 miles south of Chinle, pushing a baby carriage with a baby inside. Cooper pulled the car over. I got out and asked if she wanted a ride. She didn't say yes, she didn't even nod; she handed me the baby and began folding up the carriage. Cooper opened the trunk and helped her put it in. As soon as she was settled in the backseat, I handed her the baby. "Are you going to Ganado?" I asked. She nodded. Cooper slipped behind the wheel, eased the car forward. We purred down the empty highway. To the west, between the road and the mountains—maybe 30 miles—there was nothing but a couple of hogans, a few cattle.

I tried to make conversation then shut up. Cooper paid attention to his driving. The baby sat on the mother's lap like a doll made out of red-dark clay, round eyes staring unblinkingly into space. The day was overcast, moody...early-spring clouds concealing a last gasp of snow. We were a strange quartet bound for Ganado. The mother stared over the baby's head, between the two of us sitting in the front seat, out the window. She was a pretty woman, a trifle thickset, with strong features and sorrowful cheeks. Her eyes betrayed no eagerness to communicate, no need to warm the distance between us with idle chatter.

I reached back and stroked the baby's cheek. The baby looked at me and opened its mouth. A faint curl gathered at the corners of the mother's mouth. Cooper began to hum. ''He's a pretty baby,'' I said gallantly.

''She's a girl,'' the mother said.

Cooper laughed. The baby yawned. At the side of the road a raven pecked through the remains of an overturned bucket of Colonel Sanders' chicken.

Image Is Crossbreeding

Can we perceive two or more images simultaneously in our minds?

I thought about this one day while sitting on the rim near Tsegi Overlook.

We shift from one image to another, but it's virtually impossible to project two scenes concurrently before our inner eye. Because our manner of depicting reality is sequential, we never obtain a kaleidoscopic view of what we observe, a comprehensive overview of all the images that have gone before and those that are to appear.

While perched on the rim above White House Ruin, I would like to be able to *see* myself down there—to experience the sensation of sitting under a cottonwood while smelling the sun-drenched fragrance of the piñon trees on the rim. Simultaneity of thought and action. Fragmentation of the sensibility into sentient particles, each particle capable of registering an image, holding it in focus along with its particulars. So that the charge of a single experience is conducted through the segmented viewpoint concomitantly with others. So that we evolve toward a more vibrant organism. So that we view the canyon with the sweep of a raven *at the same time* we focus on details like the cottonwood trees across from White House Ruin.

"*Little brown lizards...*"

Little brown lizards scurry around the rim. Protective coloration on their backsides blends perfectly with the brown-red rocks of the Shinarump Conglomerate. One poked around in my shoe while I was airing my toes. When I picked it up by the tail, the air sack under its jaw puffed out in alarm.

Hunger

Back under the trees, settled in my favorite spot. Behind me, in the pasture, the sheep rag loudly at their fate. I hear the herders calling them. They make fun of the sheep, good-naturedly. The sheep don't seem to mind. Perhaps, because of their stupidity, they are comfortable creatures to be around. So passive and domesticated; so different from a truly wild animal.

I think of the buffalo and pronghorn antelope I saw one summer in the Black Hills. Buffalo are truly formidable, nappy beasts of enormous power and agility. It's no wonder they were venerated by Plains Indians. To slay a buffalo at close range with a lance or an arrow was a considerable feat. To eat the heart and liver, to chew quirts of undigested grass from its cavernous belly, was to imbue oneself with the same energy and magic.

Roasting lamb hocks over a fire isn't the same. It is a pastoral enterprise, with its own mystique surely, but nowhere as old and primeval as eating the raw parts of a slain buffalo. Today, we eat synthetic foods devoid of nourishment, unworthy of worship. From mastodons to buffalo to sheep to Big Macs. . . 30,000 years of dining on this continent.

The taste of blood, invigorated by wilderness, provides the difference. Blood on the tongue sparks images of bright animal life, a world viewed in all its detail with startling clarity. Taste delineating the eye, sharpening the focus, bringing particulars up close, defining the context. Blood into life. Life engendered by blood. Under our synthetic wrapping we harbor a paleolithic hunger.

"Another world within it lay"

Near Tsegi Overlook there's a flat rock slightly bigger than the bed of a pickup truck with a section gouged out by erosion that after a rain fills with water. In late afternoon, when the wind dies down and the air over the canyon grows still, puffy clouds are reflected on the surface of the water. You can see the shadows of passing birds, or your own face or hands if you lean over far enough. It is another way of looking at the canyon, or rather the sky over the canyon. Touch is relative but sight is oblong. If you look at anything for long enough in the proper spirit, your gaze will eventually encompass a variety of perspectives. Touch is demonstrable while sight is

Clouds reflected on water

speculative... sight includes phenomena that touch can't necessarily confirm.

The English poet Thomas Traherne once wrote an intriguing poem about pausing at the edge of a puddle and staring down at the features reflected therein. "Another world within it lay," he concluded; a different world, slightly altered, recognizable in specifics, offering yet another perspective. No doubt there is an element of narcissism here; upon any reflecting surface we hope secretly to find our own immortality confirmed, or at least our comeliness. But what of an intimate glimpse into other worlds, shapes that delight us with their unfamiliarity? Worlds as mysterious and unattainable as the Anasazi? For this we need a little artifice, the aid of a simple mirror, a surface to ricochet our thoughts off, a sling to project our visions beyond the limits of the ordinary.

Apaches de Nabahu

They came to the Southwest originally from western Canada. Athabascan-speaking people with strange habits and aggressive personalities, they filtered south over two main pathways, the east slope of the Rockies and down through the broad, sunlit uplands of the Great Basin region. Possibly they arrived as early as the 13th century to help intimidate the Anasazi into abandoning their rock-bound homes. People of enormous physical vitality and keen adaptive ability, they did not conquer other tribes so much as absorb them, incorporating key cultural features into their own social framework, augmenting and expanding and in most cases improving upon the traits they found. *Diné*, they called themselves—"the People."

The horse changed their lives, as it did the lives of many Indians on the continent. It gave them mobility, power, speed, distinction. It transformed them from a race of shaggy, foot-bound, spear hunters into a redoubtable light cavalry. The Spanish presence in the Southwest brought hardship and enslavement, but it also introduced several technological features that considerably upgraded the material life of the natives. Sheep, silvermaking, guns, tools—in addition to the horse—altered the character of the tribes and rescrambled political alliances. While the Pueblo remained sedentary, cloistered in their adobe villages, the Navajo became nomadic, wandering from range to range, mountain to mountain, in the redrock country of the Four Corners region. Because they did not live in towns, the Spanish distrusted them and referred to them as *indios bárbaros*—"wild men." There was something different about these people, something irredeemable. By taking what they wanted from other cultures, they remained uniquely themselves. By roaming the vast spaces beyond the fringe of Spanish control, they remained feral and untamed.

Long before the advent of the horse, slave trading had flourished in the Southwest. Women of child-bearing age were especially prized. Infant mortality was appalling, and one of the basic urges of any tribe, in addition to feeding itself, was to ensure its own regeneration. Fertile wombs were a vital commodity in Southwest Indian life.

By the mid-19th century Navajo warriors were renowned all over the region. They traveled long distances, terrorizing both Indians and whites. Before starting out, they purified themselves in a sweathouse. The costume they wore was different from any other tribe, indicating a distant origin, possibly the far Canadian north. Conical leather helmets of distinct Asiatic shape protected their heads; they wore doublets fashioned from three or four thicknesses of buckskin. Their arrows were dipped into a special poison extracted from the charcoal of a lightning-struck tree. They carried stone clubs and leather shields fringed with eagle feathers. The shields were dusted with a special pollen to make them resistant to enemy arrows and lances.

Every step of the warpath was regulated by taboos as to what one must eat, what position one must sleep in, what words to use when speaking. Success depended largely upon magic and good fortune. Should a coyote slink across their path, the war party would turn back. But if all signs were favorable, and they reached their target without incident, they would paint their bodies with representations of snakes and bear tracks; at dawn, amid a clatter of ululant cries, they would attack. The Hopi learned to dread the sound of that horrible *ahu ahu!* The Zuni grew increasingly bitter as their cornfields were plundered and their children kidnapped.

But the best loot was to be found in the settled communities along the Rio Grande and the ranches of Old Mexico. Two or three thousand sheep was nothing for a determined band to run off at one time. However, the raiders always left a few ewes so the Mexicans could raise another flock the following year. It was the golden age of warriordom; the world belonged to the boldest and most aggressive. Fortunes were amassed in a single raid... and lost in a counterraid. The Southwest was in upheaval, frought with martial ardor as raiders in search of plunder and glory swooped down on enemy villages. And always the finger of blame was pointed at that tribe that lived beyond the pale, that resisted the encroachments of civilization...the wild, barbaric *apaches de nabahu.*

Rabbitbrush

Rabbitbrush
blooming in puffy yellow balls

waves in the wind along South Rim Drive

The Timeless Fold

The centuries endure in the canyon, they can be perceived in the smooth rock walls, but as ''history'' here is primarily geological, they are not oppressive. Time hangs with delicate ease. So delicate, it is almost non-existent. The canyon is a timeless fold in whatever continuum we perceive as governing our lives. Time suspended, held in abeyance, intermingling with the lightsome canyon air. Wherever the earth reveals itself to any great depth there is a feeling of stasis, of time having been liberated from conventional strictures. Instead of abrading our consciousness, time nurtures it, soothes it, engenders it with solidity and awareness. In such places we experience a feeling of what it must be like to live forever. We meld our percussive, bird-like metabolism with the deepest rhythms of time.

Canyon wall

"*The air grows chill...*"

The air grows chill

●

I feel it on my bare feet

Rio de Chelly and canyon wall

Rio de Chelly

From the rim the river bed is an alluvial white band fringed with leafy trees and threaded by the mocha stain of the channel. The bed, and frequently the fields and pastures bordering it, are swept by spring floods. Floods deposit sediments brought down from the Chuska Mountains, which the current grinds and pushes toward the "chinle"—the mouth of the canyon. In such fashion the soil of the canyon is replenished. High sandy banks deflect the river's course, send it angling in new directions. The river—like all rivers—prefers the path of least resistance. Somehow, despite all obstacles, it finds a path to lower ground—in this case, the broad plain stretching west of the canyon mouth. At one time it probably drained the plain, but today it vanishes underground on the outskirts of Chinle. Mysteriously. Into the unknown.

Recurring Fantasy
I Had as a Child

Flying a kite
I remove an eyeball
attach it to the kitetail.
The optic nerve (elongated to plastic lengths)
trails down the string to the empty socket.
Looking at the kite in the air
I see myself down on the ground
                              clutching the string

Quicksand!

One morning Cooper and I tried to cross the Rio de Chelly to reach White House Ruin. It was spring, and the river was in full course, frothing from bank to bank in a pinkish swath. We took off our boots and waded out a few yards. The water rose to our calves and then to our knees. The footing underneath was squishy and uncertain. Broken sunbeams danced off the churning surface. "I don't know if we should attempt this without horses," Cooper muttered. "I think I get your drift," I replied.

The swirling water entranced me. Fed by rivulets high in the mountains, the water was ice cold, numbing my calf bones, working achy fingers deep into my groin. A specter rose up in my imagination like a hawk. Quicksand! There might be patches of quicksand somewhere in the riverbed into which we would unknowingly step. Navajos living in the canyon had reported the loss, not only of livestock, but vehicles. A scary scenario unfolded before my eyes. One false step and we would be sucked into a maw of gurgling sand that would seep into our lungs and seal our mouths and eyes and thrust us down into the bowels of the earth.

Back on the bank, drying my toes in the sparkling light, my face shadowed by a tamarisk branch, I recalled the cowboy movies I had seen in the 1940s and '50s. Particularly those with quicksand scenes. Trapped by chance or the machinations of evil outlaws, Tim Holt or Lash LaRue struggled to free themselves from a mire of gulping sand. Oh how my heart thumped as they floundered around, calling out to themselves to remain calm, reminding themselves (and the audience) that the more they struggled the quicker they would disappear. The thought of suffocating under those circumstances was worse than the thought of being tortured and shot. Sitting in a crowded theatre on a Saturday morning, munching my popcorn, listening to other kids squeal in terror, I felt my heart lurch up my throat like a frog. Of course the hero was rescued by his sidekick; or maybe he whistled to his faithful horse and the horse dangled the reins into the hero's grasping fingers and pulled him out. . . . Whatever, the specter of quicksand haunted my imagination. And even though we could probably have crossed the river, Cooper and I, of the same generation, raised on the same horse operas, elected not to. Instead, we lolled on the bank and dried our feet in the feathery air and reminisced about how we were the last generation to be influenced by this form of grade-B terror. My own children, suckled on *Star Wars* and other science fiction epics, didn't know what quicksand was; they would have splashed across the river at a gallop. But not us. Our imaginations had been molded in an earlier era. Thus are generational distinctions drawn in the postmodern world, along the thinnest of celluloid lines. Sheepish and a little embarrassed, we traded memories in giggling voices. Behind us, an animal scuttled between the olive trees along the bank. Farther back, dark and ominous, the canyon walls loomed up toward the sky like the wings of a prehistoric bird.

A Little Essay
on Rock Art

"The world in the beginning was completely real, it resounded in the human heart and with the human heart."

Antonin Artaud

Petroglyphs (pecked-out images) and picto-graphs (painted-on images) are present everywhere in the canyon. Only where desert varnish gilds the walls can you find the proper surface for pecking out images. The color of the rock underneath is lighter than the varnish, and the images, even after a thousand years, glow through the dark patina with a ghostly radiance. Unfortunately the long draperies of desert varnish descending from the rim do not always reach the canyon floor, with the result that many petroglyphs are located fairly high up, some-

Standing Cow Ruin

times in clefts or niches reachable only by minute toe- and hand-holds chipped out of sandstone. Others can be found above the ruins, and were probably incised by artists standing on the tops of pueblo towers that once were braced against the canyon walls.

Though today they seem mysterious, for the people who hacked them out the figures surely had significance. It is important to remember that many of these figures possessed an energy and power, not just to the artist, but to anyone who ran their fingers around the configurations of the incised grooves. The magic they represented was transferable in its primal charge to the beholder; it did not belong exclusively to the artist.

Rock Art: Anasazi doodling, accompanied or even overlaid in places by Navajo efforts. Side-by-side, the stylistic differences are evident. Anasazi images are stiff and rigid, while those of the Navajo (especially the pictographs) are more fluidly traced. In addition to the remarkable star panels which decorate the ceilings of caves, the Navajo excelled at reproducing historical events.

Standing Cow Ruin has a marvelous pictograph commemorating Lieutenant Narbona's march through the canyon in 1805. The pictograph shows a procession of Spanish cavalry and dogs. An armed

Indian rides with the Spaniards, while two Spaniards mounted on a single horse shoot at another Indian. The Spanish wear flat-brimmed hats and long winter capes. The lead trooper, riding a pinto, appears to have his hair arranged in a queue. Another figure—Lieutenant Narbona?—wears a black cape decorated with a white cross.

Below this painting, at the base of the cliff, are other Navajo renderings, including an almost life-sized "standing cow," horses, riders, plus a charcoal drawing of a U.S. cavalryman, c. 1860.

Anasazi Rock Art is characterized by arcane squiggles, calendric designs, and animal depictions. Their deities are also represented—masked and hooded and bewinged figures, executed in a stiff, hierarchial style, attended by creatures drawn from a multi-dimensional, cubist perspective. The religious theme is dramatized in occasional bird-like figures (human figures with avian heads), indicative, per-haps, of shamans who regularly practiced spirit flights. While in a trance, their spirits departed from their bodies, usually in the form of a bird, and soared out over the countryside.

The function of a spirit flight was not to discover new territory but rather to perceive with startling clarity the integrated wholeness of the world. Everything a shaman needed to know about the world was already evident in it—he did not have to invent or imagine this knowledge; it was already present and operable. Fundamentally, the world was an orderly place, a benevolent, life-sustaining organism whose dynamics—once tapped—were immensely powerful. Of course there was a negative side to this force, and concommitant with its healing properties was a destructive urge which could also be tapped and brought to bear upon a specific target. The key to harmony and good health was to keep the two forces in balance. And it was the shaman who was responsible for this feat; it was he who periodically had to obtain a bird's-eye perspective of the universe in order to detect and counteract pernicious influences that threatened the well-being of his people. Not only did he have to identify particulars, but he had to be able to project himself out over the entire field in order to view the field with the same specificity as he viewed a single component. The stakes were high. A great deal depended upon his acuity and breadth of vision. If he failed too often in his efforts to maintain the two opposing forces in balance, he was either banished or slain by the people.

Guy Mount, writing about the Cahuilla Indians of desert California, has suggested that elements of their rock art might have functioned as directional markers to shamans undertaking spirit flights. The same might be true of the images and patterns and designs found on the walls of Canyon de Chelly. Beyond their representative value, they might have conveyed pertinent information to airborne priests, indicating not only the location of water holes and holy sites, but paradigmatic evidence of the order of the world. Viewed on foot trudging after water or firewood, the drawings probably had a totally different meaning than when viewed during a spirit flight. A heightened perspective results in the exaltation of mundane data, whether among the Anasazi or anyone else.

The Navajo did not settle in Canyon de Chelly in any significant numbers until approximately 1750. By then the Anasazi were long gone, their diaspora having occurred most probably in the latter half of the 13th century, the result of drought, overcultivation, and encroaching enemies. Anasazi Rock Art evidently went through several different phases, the last of which (c. 1200) reflects a certain amount of turmoil and anxiety.

Navajo Rock Art is clearly demarcated into two camps, religious and secular, while Anasazi art seems less demonstrative of this schism...though, due to the absence of a lexicon or the Anasazi equivalent of a Rosetta stone, the more recondite features will remain forever beyond our comprehension. Certainly Anasazi "doodling" is more abstract and symbolic than its Navajo counterpart; a Navajo cow or horse traced on a wall is pretty much recognizable as such.

Not so Anasazi figures. While the style is fairly uniform, the interpretation is highly speculative. Which leads me to believe that the Anasazi conception of space and time was different from the Navajo. Navajo rock art includes numerous depictions of historical events. Among the Anasazi there doesn't seem to have been much of that. For them the line between temporal and cosmic was negligible. Their universe was seamless, the division between human/animal and mind/body not being particularly evident in their peckings. While individual foot and handprints might indicate a kind of personal signature, and while a deer with a spear in its chest might represent an individual triumph of sorts, it is in the representation of more exotic figures (Kokopelli, bird-headed shamans, anthropomorphic gods, etc.) that the true genius of their rock art is best revealed.

Clayton Eshleman, writing about the wall paintings of the Lascaux Cave in southwest France, says that "Paleolithic space appears to be multi-directional, not only a world of broken interrelation where everything is in association, but also a world that is not partitioned from its material by a frame or some other boundary device.'' The remark can apply to Anasazi Rock Art. There is little discrepancy between the sacred and the profane. Ordinary figures are imbued with religious significance. The Anasazi view everything simultaneously; rather than distinguishing between images according to a social or moral code, they include everything in their worldview—everything has weight and meaning and significance.

While the topography of Canyon de Chelly may have formed the limits of their physical universe, that universe was *the Universe*, a microcosm reflecting the rest of the world. Where they were, and how they lived, marked the boundaries of the material world. And while relatively stationary (compared to the Navajo), the very fact they were so remarkably *centered* enabled them to think universally. Grounded in the details of a specific terrain (Canyon de Chelly, Mesa Verde, Chaco Canyon, et al.), they were free to interpret those details in whatever fashion they wished.

For the Anasazi, identification with reality was instantaneous; no *Us* versus *Them* dichotomy seems to have prevailed. Each object had its own meaning and function in the totality of the observed world; each object had a supra-material identity as well, an attendant spirit that could (depending on how it was approached) be either beneficial or dangerous. Thus, any representation of the object in Rock Art was necessarily propitiatory—the image not only denoted the object, but its magic power as well. There was no disassociating one from the other. Outside was in. Inside was out. Every husk had a liquid core. All objects possessed a significance beyond their appearance, yet appearance was all that was required for that significance to be ascertained. The association was intuitive, as certifiable as what our own science has discovered about the interplay of protons and neutrons.

Yes, there were rickets and dysentery and cataracts and rheumatism, and a host of other ailments with few anodynes other than what a handful of boiled herbs could provide or the mesmeric therapy of an eagle feather. At the same time there was that vision—the ability to see straight through the universe, from front to back, not in a wide, representative spectrum, but rather in a tight narrow cone of tribal perception. It wasn't the Entire Universe that the Anasazi perceived, it was more like a slice or section. (Synecdoche? Canyon de Chelly standing for all other canyons? All other possible landscapes?) Because it was all part of one fractureless, intricately webbed experience—one totality—it was enough; it was *everything*.

"No wind stirs
the cottonwoods..."

No wind stirs the cottonwoods. Silence is total. The sheep have left the pasture behind me and bawled their way downstream, out of sight, out of earshot.

The light under the trees has begun to pale. The wall rising above White House Ruin, streaked with desert varnish, is slowly being rinsed of sunlight. This evening the smooth sandstone will glow with residual intensity. Tonight, it will give off a dull, spectral radiance.

No wind stirs the cottonwoods. The sun touches the rim.

Time, perhaps, for an epiphany... a lucid revelation?

Just this moment—in all its placidity and calm— will do.

Synopsis for an
Unwritten Novel

Man and woman, married sixteen years, come
to Canyon de Chelly, accompanied by the woman's
father, a retired history professor. The woman is a
photographer, the man a poet. He has published
widely, but with little recognition. They both have
been to the canyon before, the professor too, many
times. In fact he has come there (hopefully) to die.
He is an old man, sick with cancer, nearly blind with
cataracts, and he wants, against his daughter's
wishes, to spend the night in the canyon, listening to
the wind swish the cottonwoods, the river swirl over
the sandy floor. (The time is early June.) He once
wrote a history of the Navajo, which now, in his

infirmity, he realizes was wrong, not so much in fact as in spirit. In it he exonerated Kit Carson as a military commander, the fact that he accomplished so much with so few casualties, Navajo or Anglo. Wrapped in a blanket purchased decades before at the Hubbell Trading Post, he walks (accompanied by his family) down White House Trail, settles for the night near the river, at the edge of a pasture, under a brushy canopy of tamarisks. The daughter parts with him reluctantly. She's afraid he'll take a chill or be trampled by grazing sheep. The son-in-law thinks the old man magnificently dotty. He admires his eyeballs, puffed and rounded like tufts of Johnson & Johnson cotton, magnified behind tortoise-shell lenses that make the old man look brainy and ascetic. He has his own objective for the evening. While the old man, swaddled in woven sheep's wool, communes with the gods that drift between the canyon walls, up on the rim, on top of another blanket (this purchased in the Atlas Mountains outside Marrakech), he and his wife make love. As he enters her, a ripple of delight courses up his spine. The sensation is as intense as any he has ever experienced. The gaping width of the canyon seems to yawn voluptuously under pressure of the passion that surges through his body. Attracted by the commotion, a pipestrelle bat flutters over his head.

81

A full moon rises over the Chuska Mountains, inking deep shadows under the canyon rim. The exhalation of their breath intensifies over the hiss of the evening wind through the piñon trees. They have thought about this for a long time. They discussed it briefly in the car on the way to Chinle. It is their way of making a prayer to the canyon, of demonstrating the effect the place has on them, of dramatizing the affection and yearning they feel.

And more—but it is the woman who thinks this more forcefully than the man; she believes that what they are doing is only a beginning. This act of communion, of mingling their desire with their bodily fluids, of reaching through one another to a more solvent reality, is merely a prelude to the real work ahead. The canyon is like an intagliated battery pack that gives off numinous energy convertible by attentive people into a generative force. The woman believes this implicitly. So does her husband, whose cries of delight splash off her cheeks and face like drops from a mossy fountain. We must take this energy and radiate it out to the ends of the earth, she thinks. We must. We must. Two or three people with healthy bodies and generous hearts can turn the tide of human thought, can redirect catalytic flashes to clarify the world of muddled desire and negative urges.

Moonrise over canyon

Delirium mounts in the man's eyes on little expostulations of joy. I love you, he whispers. I love you   I love you   I love you

The woman's imagination glows like the tip of a succulent cigar. The canyon seems to wrap its walls around her like a brace of tender arms. There is power here, she thinks, that we can never tap in a thousand lifetimes. Stored energy from the sun. Two or three people, assembled together in the name of sanity and good sense, can redirect the force of the canyon's healing grace back out into the world. They can   They can

The two dissolve in a rapture of passionate kisses. Meanwhile, down below, the old man, visions of Kit Carson and burning peach orchards igniting his brain, issues antiquated military commands in a creaky voice that spirals up like smoke and disappears.

"*No self-pity. . .*"

No self-pity
If I die now
hopefully my body will serve as fodder
for varmints & ravens
        Destiny : to have one's corporeal parts
subsumed in the Earth

    ample fare for plants & scavengers

Little Kit

For decades the Navajos raided Pueblo and Hispanic settlements in New Mexico. Adroit thieves, they ran off cattle and horses and kidnapped women and children. Retaliation, at best, was desultory. A Pueblo expedition would enter Navajo territory, burn a few hogans, kill a few warriors, capture a few women and children. Back and forth the two sides went, looting and pillaging, neither side achieving sufficient leverage to overpower the other.

And then, in 1846, the Americans arrived.

Out in Navajoland their presence was barely felt. The Navajos, hemmed in by enemies on all sides—Pueblo and Hispanic to the east, Zunis to the south, Hopis to the west, Utes to the north—sallied forth at will from their eerie redrock country to ignite fires all over the Colorado Plateau. A populous tribe of some 8,000 people, they were reported to be well-off, having at their disposal many sheep, cattle, cornfields, and orchards. By the 1860s it was evident that only a sound thrashing would curb their marauding habits.

Brigadier General James Carleton, Kit Carson's superior, was chosen for the job. With the proper application of force, he felt he could convince the Navajo to leave off their warrior ways and settle into a life of agricultural repose. Like many 19th-century Christian military men, Carleton felt the solution to the Indian problem was to turn them into yeoman farmers—dusky prototypes of the Jeffersonian ideal—replete with mule, plow, bib overalls, and straw hat.

In the summer of 1863 Kit Carson went out to Arizona at the head of a mixed force of Hispanic, American, and Pueblo soldiers. Accompanying him, eager to score revenge, were Ute, Hopi, and Zuni scouts. For every Navajo horse they killed or captured, Kit paid $20; for every sheep, a dollar. A handsome bounty was also paid for every dead Navajo. It was war at its scummiest. The Navajos were too wily to show themselves in force, so instead of ferreting them out Kit decided to destroy their source of food. Proceeding through Canyon de Chelly from west to east, he burned everything in sight, trampled fields, shot everything that moved. Navajos on the rim or atop monoliths like Fortress Rock jeered at the invaders, but not for long. Little Kit knew how to wage war. A total of 50 Navajo warriors were slain. The troops were pleased with the minimal number of casualties on both sides. In January snow descended, bitter cold tightened against the sandstone walls. What will it take to make you go away? wondered the Navajo elders. Come to me, said Kit, lay down your arms, and renounce your land. But you are asking us to give up everything! the elders protested. Do that, said Kit, or I will kill every one of you.

Contemporary daguerreotypes show a diminutive man with a wide forehead, receding hair, squinty eyes, and pinched mouth. For nearly 40 years, ever since jumping a tannery apprenticeship back in Missouri, Kit had been prowling the Southwest. His attitude toward Indians was sympathetic yet ribbed with steel. His first wife had been Arapaho. When she died after the birth of their daughter, he was distraught. And yet, while he might cultivate them personally, as a white man—a representative of his culture—he viewed them as an obstacle in the March of Progress. There was no tolerating their presence; either they adapted or died.

All that he had learned from Indians about

Fortress Rock

tracking and hunting and reading a landscape and knowing what shrubs contain healing properties and what month the animals went into hiding, all these practical yet magical bits of information he employed against the Navajo that terrible winter of 1863-64. The lesson paid off handsomely, though Kit was largely unappreciative of the gift. His mental faculties did not include a keen sensitivity to irony. Representative of the pragmatic side of the 19th-century sensibility, he did what he had to do to get the job done. General Carleton praised him extravagantly. Some Navajos still choke at the mention of his name.

Without food, freezing, the old ones perishing in the snow, the Navajos finally came in, a few at a time, then more and more, finally in the hundreds. In the spring of 1864 (at approximately the same time that, back east, Grant was cranking up the Army of the Potomac to assault Lee), the captives were herded 300 miles to the Bosque Redondo, a treeless plain in east-central New Mexico. The memory of that grueling hegira still haunts Navajo consciousness, and is known by them as ''the Long Walk.'' Hundreds of people died just getting there; scavengers fed off their hastily buried bodies.

At the Bosque Redondo they were given seed and a few implements, but the soil was too alkaline to produce a sizeable harvest. The first year a cut-worm infestation destroyed the corn crop. Unable to obtain adequate supplies from the U.S. Government, the Navajos starved and froze to death in hovels dug out along the banks of the Pecos River. From his headquarters in Albuquerque General Carleton wrote consolingly, "Tell the Navajo to be too proud to murmur at what cannot be helped..."

Thrown together with captive Apaches, the two tribes, though linguistically related, were constantly at odds. To make matters worse, their lack of arms made them easy prey for raiding Comanches and Kiowas, who ran off the little stock they had and destroyed their fields. Soldiers at nearby Fort Stanton, understaffed and ill-equipped, proved ineffective at protecting their charges. The cost of maintaining the tribe in this barren ground eventually proved more than even the U.S. Government was willing to pay. In 1868 the Navajo were allowed to return to their homeland in northeast Arizona.

Against rival Indians the Navajos were fearsome, though like most Southwest tribes they were less than adequate when pitted against white soldiers. The difference had nothing to do with individual valor, but rather with superior technology and organization, which the whites enjoyed and the Navajo didn't. The U.S. Army in the field also was not burdened by the presence of women, children, and old people. Kit Carson brought a concept of total war to Navajoland, antedating the way wars would be fought in the next century. Southwest tribes raided one another incessantly, they kidnapped non-hostiles, looted, and burned, but they did not, as did Carson, systematically destroy the economic and social foundations of their enemies. (Not only was such a concept alien to them, they possessed neither the technology nor manpower to implement it.) Almost a year before William Tecumseh Sherman marched through Georgia to the sea, Kit Carson marched through the heart of the Navajo nation, scourging the very base from which that nation operated. It makes you wonder if Sherman ever read Carson's dispatches. As nasty as it sometimes was, war to an Indian was more like a contest, a game. Ironically, there was something medieval about it, similar to the jousting between knights. Carson completely subverted that principle by bringing to bear upon the Navajo (with the force of a mailed fist) a totally different method of warfare, one aimed not so much at the warrior caste as at the entire culture. To be sure, he stopped short of genocide; yet what he had in mind (as did Carleton) was clearly a form of cultural genocide—the replacement of one way of life with another.

Upon arriving in the Southwest in 1846, the U.S. Army attacked the tribes individually—Pueblo, Mescalero Apache, Navajo, Apache—and slowly ground them into submission. Think how much stickier Kit Carson's job would have been had the Utes, say, leagued themselves with the Navajo...had any of the Southwest tribes presented a united confederation against the bluecoats. Once Canyon de Chelly was subdued, Carson would have had to strike north into the Four Corners region. Pulled deeper and deeper into that weird and marvelous country, farther and farther from his supply bases, sniped at incessantly, his flanks harassed by dogged braves, searching for an enemy that could vanish with ease into a maze of tangled canyons, he might have spent years trying to bring the Indians to bay. Instead, for a few dollars, plus a promise to keep all the captives they seized, the Utes led Carson to every Navajo stronghold they could find.

Navajo Tacos

Navajo tacos tumble off the coal chute at Black Mesa
steamy chunks of Navajo taco
fry bread   onions   green pepper   pinto beans
grainy bits of hamburger meat chugging down the
                                    Peabody conveyor belt
instead of chunks of coal.
Instead of tumbling into railroad cars bound for the
                                    power plant
at Page to feed electricity to desert cities
choked with RVs chromed with minerals
extracted from the moon
Navajo tacos tumbling into Navajo mouths.
Instead of coal dug up from the earth to churn
                                    the turbines

at the Navajo Power Plant
to pump electricity to condominiums in Phoenix
peopled by midwesterners clad in polyester
with butched hair & vinous cheeks
who suck the spotty Colorado dry with silver-plated
                                                straws
Navajo tacos scooped up by dozers & steam shovels
& ladled into the mouths of hungry Navajo   hungry
Ethiopians   hungry Hindustani   hungry Somalis
whose teeth revenge the ravaged face of Black Mesa,
grind the implements of Peabody-extracting
                              corporations
into tiny excretory bits. . .

"Dragonflies observe..."

Dragonflies observe the world through polygonally-lensed eyes, each eye perceiving a slightly different image, all eyes perceiving a composite portrait, varying in particulars, identifiable in outline.

To stand in the middle of a field and be aware of the activities in the grass around you, at the same time to remain cognizant of what's going on in the trees at either end—the animal movements, plant disposition, wind velocity, temperature fluctuations, etc.

To see the whole world as clearly as a man can see the ground between his feet.

Kokopelli

You see the incised images on rock surfaces all over the Southwest. A humpbacked figure like a turtle, with antennae pronging off the head, a stick or what appears to be a flute protruding from the face. Kokopelli. The great Amerindian fertility symbol. God—or goddess?—of fecundity and harvest.

What guarantee did its presence grant to both creator and beholder? If we draw the figure of a god, if we delineate its image, will it ensure us a full and healthy life? Is the act of summoning the deity's form sufficient to inspire it to function on our behalf? How does this process work?

There are representations that depict Kokopelli's

Kokopelli and rock art

hump loaded with little zeroes symbolizing seeds. A hermaphroditic figure, embodying male and female reproductive functions. A divine figure, yet provocatively human. Reportedly, it originated with the Hohokam in southern Arizona and was later adapted by the Anasazi. There is no more stirring image in all Southwest Rock Art. The sight of it always makes me feel good, like one of Bruegel's harvest paintings depicting peasants scything hay on a hot afternoon. The image stirs thoughts of harvest, fulfillment, and fruition. Kokopelli is the Native American version of the Orphic myth. He heals at the same time he nourishes. He discharges seeds at the same time he incubates them inside his body. He is every mystic's dream of meaningful androgyny. He is the idealization of the Native American belief that the human form harbors both male and female characteristics, and that, in order to satisfy Nature's urge, both must be acknowledged and expressed.

The sight of the figure scratched upon a palette of desert varnish can be catalytic. You hear a kind of music, high-pitched and quavery, inside your head. Kokopelli is a genitalized expression of the desire of all people to be fruitful and multiply, not just in numbers but in spirit. The sound of his imaginary flute recalls a time when the mere exhalation of breath in the form of a suggestive word had the power to call into being an entirely new object or idea. Kokopelli is the oldest and most potent muse ever formulated upon this continent. Poets should carry the image around their necks on a chain and hold it close to their hearts at all times.

Touch is relative but sight is oblong

I realized something this morning on the rim. In order to write about what I had seen I had to turn away from it, to create a private reserve in which I could summon up a version of what I had witnessed, uninfluenced by the actual sight. The stepping back or turning away from (turning away from the object under scrutiny, into myself, so to speak) was critical to the process of recording it on paper. We live by confrontation; however, in order to reproduce the experience we must assess it obliquely, from the side, in intuitive flashes. The world is meant to be observed from the shadowy depths of a small cave, peering out through an opening that widens and narrows to the rhythm of the light generated within.

"On my belly at Sliding House Overlook..."

On my belly at Sliding House Overlook, crawling forward, I finally reach the rim, peer carefully over. The canyon wall drops straight down for a thousand feet; at the bottom I see a hogan and a cornfield. A dirt track snakes past the hogan, following the bend of the river. Nearby, on a grassy slope, a herd of sheep grazes. Across the river, spilling down the face of the North Wall, are several rock slides supporting the remains of Anasazi dwellings.

The space below beckons temptingly. Not that I care to jump, but rather that I long to fly off these rocks and wing over the river. To be a bird at

Canyon de Chelly would be a pleasant fate. To see down into the canyon while viewing the humps of the Chuska Mountains. To watch the river crinkle past steep cutbanks while basking in cloud shadows.

Like most canyons on the Colorado Plateau, Canyon de Chelly suggests a dimension beyond the conventional, an other-worldliness, an arena where different physical laws obtain. Things occur here that simply can't on top. No doubt there's a ''lost kingdoms'' mentality implicit in this statement, yet another illustration of the fundamental dislocation of the western psyche. We sense that life down there is simpler and therefore better, which may be nothing more than a pastoral fallacy, the nostalgic affection Anglos routinely express for picturesque scenes.

It hasn't always been that way. Before we converted it into a postcard, the wilderness was our enemy. Our European ancestors in the 17th century regarded it as a malevolent force. All those trees! A gloomy darkness unrelieved by the flailing of an ax! How far west did they have to forge before they encountered a clearing where they could at last breathe freely? Given the polarized cast of their minds, it's no wonder they saw phantoms in the leaves, heard Satan mouthing blasphemies through the menstrual blood of their wives. Life on this continent was a Beast to be Subdued, the starch removed, the sinew to be corded into harnessing for stubborn mules.

For all its allure, the canyon remains beyond reach, a Platonic abstract embodying eternal virtues, or perhaps a whisper of a former Atlantis, a place where we once lived in simple harmony. Though we can imagine a life down there, we can never recreate the original conditions responsible for the character of that life. Nonetheless, in stubborn New World fashion, we must attempt to make the identification; and the way to do so is to break down the dichotomy between Them and Us—aboriginals versus arrivistes, natives versus settlers. To be sure, the Navajo living in the canyon are different from us—racially, by customs, habits, and traditions; however, we share common feelings and a common fate. And while we may not be able to share the therapeutic benefits of their rituals, we can learn a lot about how to live from observing the manner in which they address their fellow creatures. Lacking an instinctive kinship with the land, fearful that the link-up may exist somewhere outside ourselves, we chew the cud of a fretful anxiety, one that threatens to consume us with its mindless demands. Our penchant for singularity, for configuring ourselves as separate and distinct entities, makes it difficult to submerge ourselves in the canyon. We lost the ability long ago when we ceased studying the entrails of animals and started to rely upon the Corn Gods to nourish us with their myths. The mystery of animal blood contains secrets undisclosable through any other medium. Our real Fall was not from Eden, certainly not the sanitized, viperless Garden that Christian fundamentalists would have us believe. Rather, it was a fall from a bloody animal past, bound up with the hunt and other rituals, and our subsequent estrangement from creatures without whom, body and soul, we could not possibly have survived.

Get off the rim and down into the canyon. That's the first step toward dissolving the barriers between ourselves and the delimiting concept of *Other*. Get out into the land, hunker down into it. The Navajo emergence myth describes a series of upward maneuvers through various worlds by the likes of Coyote and Spider Woman and First Man into increasingly complicated levels of consciousness. By reversing the process, by stepping into the land and probing deeper, we can encounter emotional and spiritual realms denied to us by a materialist culture. A canyon is a pouch or fold, a vast geologic kiva, leading to the heart of the Earth. At the bottom, shaped by the need to envelop our lives in durable myth, lies the sipapu down through which we must squeeze. Everything we need to know can be found there. In that depth merge personal longing and ancestral memories. In that depth we can finally— without restraint or self-consciousness—celebrate the Earth, the tenuous yet vital links that bind us to her.

"*The mosquitoes have found me...*"

The mosquitoes have found me

•

It's time to go

Postlude:
Leo Brown

It was dusk when I started up the trail to the rim. The sun had disappeared, taking with it the powerful colors that had suffused the canyon with light. Under the bower of tamarisk and Russian olive trees, the air was gray and almost cold. . .not a good place to spend the night, I thought with a shiver. The de Chelly sandstone shone with a dull brown sheen as if someone had sponged it clean.

I had just emerged from a tunnel cut through an overhanging rock near the foot of the trail when I heard a voice. A quiet voice like a child alone in a room babbling to itself.

From around a boulder came a Navajo—a small man with square shoulders, a round face, and thick chest. He walked with a rolling, pigeon-toed gait. He wore jeans, blue sneakers, a tattered sweatshirt, and a knitted sailor's watchcap. In his hand he carried a bright yellow shopping bag.

"Hola! Ha!" he greeted, slowing his pace.

"Hello."

"Yes...and you...Hola! And where have you been today?"

The voice was strong and lusty, the words slurred and difficult to catch.

"Down in the canyon," I replied. "At White House Ruin."

"Did you see any Anasazi?" he said with a snort, nearly choking on the backwash of his own joke.

"No, only tourists."

"Yes, tourists...ha! They bring money... money."

"Where have you been?" I asked politely.

"Me? Well, you know..." He stuck his thumb out like a hitchhiker. "There. Over there. Chinle."

I pointed at the yellow shopping bag. "Looks like you bought some things."

"Food!" he boomed. "Drink!" Then he cocked his head and peered at me closely. "I live here. Right down here."

"In the canyon," I nodded.

"Yes...yes. Right over there!"

He gestured toward the tunnel. At the foot of the trail, behind a screen of tamarisk trees, was a hogan—a squat, eight-sided structure made of logs and clay chinking with a domed earth roof from which sprouted a few dry blades of grass. I had seen it on my way down into the canyon and thought it looked abandoned.

"So you live there, eh?"

His eyes narrowed. They were small eyes, warm and appealing, chiseled out of deep slots under a blunt forehead. His long cheeks sloped to a pudgy jaw and pointed chin.

"Leo Brown."

"Pardon?"

"Me. That's me. Leo Brown."

"Oh, yeah...okay. Hey, how are you?"

I introduced myself, and we shook hands. He kept hold of my hand. His palm felt warm and calloused against mine.

"You Republican? Democrat?"

The question startled me. Granted, it was an election year, but I didn't expect to be asked that question by a Navajo near the bottom of Canyon de Chelly.

"Democrat."

"Ha...ha! Ha ha ha ha ha..."

"What about you?"

"Kayendee..."

"Pardon?"

"Ka-yen-dee! Ka-yen-dee!"

"Who?"

"Bobby! John!"

"Kennedy!" I practically shouted.

"Ha! Yes. Kayendee!"

"Well...yes...sure...Kennedy."

"Kayendee...President!"

"It would be nice, wouldn't it?"

"I'm Catholic," Leo said proudly, poking a thumb at his chest. "I am a medicine man, too."

"Really?"

"Kayendee..."

"So you live down here," I said, nodding toward the tunnel.

"Leo...I am Leo Brown!"

"Yes, Leo...well, hello again."

"I am Catholic...a medicine man."

He squeezed my hand and grabbed hold of my wrist and squeezed it. His eyes were juiced and bloodshot, the irises like dull pennies flecked around the rims with tiny red spots.

"I am a veteran...World War II. MacArthur ...the Pacific."

"No kidding."

111

"Saipan. I was at Iwo, too. First Marines. Leo Brown."

"Wow. Well, that certainly is something to be proud of."

"Soldier...powpowpow." He raised a fist and rapped at the evening air with his knuckles. "I live down here now."

"It's quite a place, Leo. I'm sure you never tire of it."

"Kayendee..." His voice was melancholy.

"I wish he were still alive," I said.

Leo gripped my elbow with his other hand. "Me and you...let's us vote for Kayendee."

His voice trembled. His face lit up. The muddy film vanished from his eyes.

"Good idea," I replied.

"Kayendee..."

"He was a great one."

"You vote...I vote...*two* votes!"

"Wonderful!"

"Leo Brown..."

And then he pulled me toward him and wrapped his arms around my shoulders. In a gesture of clumsy affection we embraced, two lonely figures at the foot of a long, steep trail, with darkness stealing up out of the canyon, rising like a tide pool around our ankles. I was a half head taller. His arm clung tightly to my neck, pulling my cheek down against his. His bristly skin rubbed affectionately against mine. We were like two walruses nuzzling one another on an isolated rock far out to sea. We remained that way for several moments. When we pulled apart his eyes were teary and his thin lips quivered.

"It was good to meet you, Leo" I said in a tight voice.

He glanced down, then back up, his eyes like two fish angling for a different hook. "You maybe... you maybe have a dollar for me?"

"Sure."

I dug into my pocket, took out several bills.

"Thanks. Thank you."

I gave him one, then another, then stuffed the wad in his hand. "Keep them," I mumbled.

"Kayendee..."

We embraced again, shook hands, drew back stiffly, self-consciously, patting each other on the arm.

"Take care of yourself, Leo."

"Yes...yes. I live here! Right down here in that hogan!"

"It's a great place, Leo. Thanks for sharing it with me."

We backed off, turned, and started off in our respective directions. Leo commenced to babble again, his voice rising and falling in a singsong chant as he sauntered down the trail. I began the long trudge up; at the next switchback I turned and looked back. Leo stood in front of the tunnel entrance. The dark, creeping up off the canyon floor like a presence, seemed poised to swallow him up. The yellow shopping bag sparked about his leg like a firefly. He waved at me. "Kayendee!" he called. "Kayen*dee!*"

His voice rang jubilantly along the sandstone walls.

"Ka-yen-dee!" I shouted back.

Hogan and full moon

Publications by Sweetlight Books
Box 307, Arcata CA 95521

Copies of our books can be ordered by mail. Please fill out the order form provided on the reverse side of this page.

Not For Innocent Ears $7.95
Spiritual Traditions of a Desert Cahuilla
Medicine Woman, 1980.
By Ruby Modesto and Guy Mount
Revised Edition, 1986
ISBN: 0-9604462-0-6

The Peyote Book $8.95
A Study of Native Medicine, 1987.
Compiled and Edited by Guy Mount
Second Edition, 1988.
ISBN: 0-9604462-3-0

Canyon de Chelly $8.95
The Timeless Fold, 1988.
By Conger Beasley, Jr.
ISBN: 0-9604462-4-9

Lady Ocean $3.00
A Love Story for Children, 1986.
By Guy Mount
ISBN: 0-9604462-2-2

How Steelhead Lost His Stripes $3.00
A Children's Story and Coloring Book, 1984.
By Guy Mount
ISBN: 0-9604462-1-4

Sweetlight Books
ORDER FORM

Name _____

Address _____

City/State/Zip _____

Qty.	Title	Cost
____	NOT FOR INNOCENT EARS	$_____
____	THE PEYOTE BOOK	_____
____	CANYON DE CHELLY	_____
____	HOW STEELHEAD LOST HIS STRIPES	_____
____	LADY OCEAN	_____

Subtotal $_____

SAVE: 20% discount on 2 books,
30% on 3, 40% on 4,
50% on 5 or more . . . .(–_____)

Subtotal $_____

California residents add 6% tax _____

Postage and handling $__2.00__

TOTAL $_____

Thanks kindly for your order.
Please send this form with your payment to:
SWEETLIGHT BOOKS
Box 307
Arcata, CA 95521